'Til Golf Do Us Part

by Fred H. Thomas

Design by Lisa Kronauer

Spectacle Lane Press

Fred Thomas:

Fred Thomas is probably the only architect who became a cartoonist and then the only cartoonist who became an architect and excelled in both apparently unrelated fields.

He graduated from Cornell University with a degree in architecture in 1957, and , although newly married, decided to draw cartoons instead of plans for a living.

He sold his first cartoon to TV Guide for $50, and made numerous subsequent sales to top markets. In 1960 he achieved every cartoonist's dream—national syndication—creating a sports panel, LONG SHOTS, for Hall Syndicate that ran in leading newspapers for six years.

Facing the reality of supporting a growing family, Thomas went back to architecture full-time in 1966 and in the next 29 years built a 150-person architectural/engineering firm with offices in three states.

Retiring to Martha's Vineyard, Massachusetts, in 1995, Thomas, proving that he hadn't lost his sense of humor during his years as a full-time architect, returned to cartooning, and resumed selling to major markets as if he had never left the drawing board.

THIS HAS TO BE MY WIFE'S FAULT!

THE AUTHOR DOING RESEARCH FOR THE BOOK

Since Thomas and his wife Ting (a former club champion) have played a lot of golf together, his first book 'Til Golf Do Us Part is not autobiographical. As the book shows, however, he missed few opportunities to observe the ongoing battle of the sexes between other golfing husbands and their exasperated non-golfing wives.

Published by Spectacle Lane Press, Inc.
P.O. Box 1237
Mt. Pleasant, SC 29465-1237
ISBN 0-930753-23-2

Published simultaneously in the United States
and Canada.

Printed in the United States of America.

To Ting, my club champion,
with love

Introduction

Golf widows aren't really widows, but they might as well be if they are married to an obsessed golfer, who is somewhat different from a normal golfer, although the difference is primarily one of degree.

Normal golfers play once or twice a week at most and sometimes give their family relations priority over their golf. Obsessed golfers, on the other hand, spend little time at home, and are seldom present for family occasions such as birthdays, weddings and funerals. They think, talk, and live golf 24 hours a day; and would rather win a 25-cent Nassau than the Nobel Prize.

Golf widows wage a constant struggle to change all of this, to get their men back and save their homes and marriages; but, like any addiction, the dependency on golf is hard to break. Their wives constantly harangue them, but it doesn't seem to have any effect, since obsessed golfers are deaf to any suggestions that they cut down on their golf.

Golf widows, who need all the support they can get, at long last have a champion in cartoonist and golfer, Fred Thomas. At the risk of being considered a traitor to his fellow male golfers, he strikes some hefty blows for oppressed golf widows everywhere in this lively, funny no-holds-barred book.

Through some 100 on-target cartoons, Fred Thomas exposes obsessed golfers for what their wives say they are—preoccupied, adolescent oafs, who should be home doing something important like fixing leaky faucets rather than chasing a little white ball across a meadow.

He also offers some suggestions for shaming and shocking the straying spouses back into line. These include moving out with the furniture and the kids while the golf-happy mate is away playing; running over his clubs with the car; putting his bed out in the yard; or, in a final act of desperation, whacking him over the head with his three-iron.

Golf widows, will get a lot of laughs and satisfaction from this book. But Fred Thomas handles the whole obsessed golfer/golf widow conflict with such good nature that even hardened obsessive golfers will be able to laugh at themselves. They might even mend their ways, which would bring peace to the old homestead and be somewhat less expensive than the divorce court.

" I'M PRAYING FOR AN EARLY SPRING."

10

IT'S THE THOUGHT THAT COUNTS

"YOU'RE RIGHT, GEORGE...A BIG BERTHA DRIVER PROBABLY ISN'T SOMETHING I WOULD HAVE GOTTEN FOR MYSELF FOR MY BIRTHDAY."

"ACTUALLY, YOU BEING STUCK IN A POT-BUNKER SOUNDS RIGHT TO ME, GEORGE."

" THE GOLF TOURNAMENT WENT TO EXTRA HOLES, GEORGE DIDN'T. "

"I FIGURE IT COMES TO ABOUT $5800 AN OUNCE, NOT COUNTING GREENS FEES."

" AND YOU, MR. RAFFERTY .... DO YOU HAVE A PREFERENCE ON LOCATION ?"

" ANYTHING TO KEEP ME FROM PLAYING GOLF ON WEEKENDS, RIGHT, ELEANOR ?"

"IF YOU REALLY WANT TO LEARN HOW TO PLAY GOLF, JOHNNY, WATCH EVERYTHING YOUR FATHER DOES AND DO THE OPPOSITE."

" I DON'T UNDERSTAND, SUSAN, IF YOU'RE THE
JEALOUS TYPE WHY DIDN'T YOU SAY SO BEFORE WE
GOT MARRIED. "

"YOU'VE BEEN TELLING THE FLOODS ALL THE DETAILS ABOUT YOUR HOLE-IN-ONE HAVEN'T YOU, GEORGE,"

" GUESS WHAT, MOTHER, I FINALLY PERSUADED HAROLD TO GIVE UP GOLF. "

"THEN IT'S AGREED...NOT MORE THAT TWO PEOPLE TALKING WHILE ANYONE IS MAKING A SHOT."

" THE REAL TREAT COMES WHEN MR. TOBIN PAYS YOU $20°° TO GET THEM BACK. "

"I'M REALLY ADJUSTING TO RETIREMENT VERY WELL ... HOW ABOUT YOU, GRACE ?"

"I DON'T THINK YOU UNDERSTAND, ALICE, I WORK AND I PLAY GOLF. I DON'T HAVE ANY LEISURE TIME."

"DO YOU HAVE ANY 'EITHER THE GOLF CHANNEL GOES OR I GO' CARDS?"

" WHEN YOU SUGGESTED THAT WE GET A BURIAL PLOT AND TOMBSTONES SO THAT THE KEY MEMBERS OF THE FAMILY COULD BE TOGETHER FOR ALL TIME, JOE......."

" IT SEEMS THAT THEIR DYNASTY WAS RIGHT ON
THE VERGE OF CONQUERING THE WORLD WHEN THE
PHARAOH DISCOVERED THAT IF HE HIT A SMALL
WHITE DIMPLED BALL WITH A CLUB...."

" ... AND WHEN YOU HIT YOUR HUSBAND WITH THE THREE WOOD, MRS. WILLIAMSON ..... DID YOU USE AN INTERLOCKING OR OVERLAPPING GRIP ? "

" HEADS I PLAY EIGHTEEN HOLES AT THE CLUB,
TAILS I HIT BALLS AND PLAY NINE HOLES AND IF
IT STANDS ON EDGE I STAY HOME AND HELP
WITH THE GARDENING .... "

" ISN'T LIFE FUNNY, ALICE? YOU'RE SICK IN BED ALL DAY AND I'M THE ONE WHO SEES THE DOCTOR ALL DAY."

" HAVE YOU EVER GIVEN MUCH THOUGHT TO WHAT YOU WANT TO BE WHEN YOU GROW UP, GEORGE ? "

" WIPE THAT TRIPLE-BOGIE OFF YOUR FACE, SON! "

" I CERTAINLY HOPE YOU'RE NOT GOING TO GIVE ME A LOT OF STATIC ABOUT MY PLAYING AN EXTRA NINE HOLES WITH THE GUYS, GRACE ! "

" HE CAN'T COME OUT AND PLAY UNTIL HE FINISHES MY HOMEWORK. "

"GUESS,"

" THAT'S NICE, DEAR . WHAT'S A HOLE-IN-ONE ? "

"...AND THIS IS THE PITCHING WEDGE HE WRAPPED AROUND A TREE ON THE 18TH AT PEBBLE BEACH IN '87."

" FOR CRIPES SAKE, ALICE, COULDN'T THIS WAIT
' TIL TREVINO PUTTS OUT. "

"TOUGH DAY AT THE GOLF COURSE, RALPH?"

"THE KIDS WON'T FALL ASLEEP, GEORGE. WOULD YOU MIND COMING UP TO TELL THEM ABOUT YOUR GOLF GAME."

"...AND THIS IS THE GOLF TROPHY THAT GEORGE PICKED UP IN 1991...AT A YARD SALE."

" FOR GOD'S SAKE, DON'T ASK HIM ABOUT HIS HOLE-IN-ONE ! "

" I'M SURE THAT BEING A GOLF WIDOW CAN BE VERY
PAINFUL, MRS JOHNSON, BUT I'M AFRAID THAT WHEN
IT COMES DOWN TO COLLECTING ON A LIFE INSURANCE
POLICY..... "

"ONLY GOLF TROPHY CHARLIE EVER EARNED!"

"DON'T BE RIDICULOUS, ALICE. HOUSES DON'T CATCH FIRE DURING THE FINAL ROUND OF THE MASTERS."

"I'M NOT REALLY WORRIED ABOUT IT, WHEN HE LEARNS TO WRITE AND KEEP SCORE HE'LL PROBABLY GIVE IT UP,"

" ONE LAST WORD OF ADVICE, DEAR. IF HE DOESN'T TELL YOU HIS GOLF SCORE, DON'T ASK. "

" WELL, IT'S CERTAINLY NICE TO SEE YOU, MR. JONES.
WIFE HIDE YOUR GOLF CLUBS AGAIN ? "

"...AND FOR AN EXTRA $3.00 PER MONTH I CAN INSTALL THIS LITTLE SWITCH THAT WILL PREVENT **RECEPTION** OF ESPN AND THE GOLF CHANNEL."

"YOU MEAN THAT'S ALL YOU HAVE TO SHOW,"
FOR A WHOLE SUMMER ON THE GOLF COURSE!

" SAY, ALICE, ... BERNIE TELLS ME THAT HE READ IN THE BIRTH ANNOUNCEMENTS THAT WE HAD A BABY BOY LAST WEEK.... "

" I THINK THE ONLY WAY I CAN GET GEORGE'S UNDIVIDED ATTENTION IS TO DRESS LIKE A GOLF BALL. "

"MOM KEEPS HOPING HE'LL GROW UP SOME DAY."

" I'M GOING TO HAVE TO REFER YOU TO
DR. KUSICK. HE HAS A LATER TEE OFF TIME."

" I JUST GOT WORD THAT MY MOTHER IS VERY SICK.
CAN I HAVE THE REST OF THE DAY OFF ? "

" LADIES' TEE . "

" MIND IF I HAVE A LITTLE PEEK AT THE RULE
    BOOK, CHARLIE ? "

" COME ON, GEORGE, PLAY FAIR! THAT'S NOT FORE
YOU'VE HIT THE BALL AT LEAST SIX TIMES! "

" I UNDERSTAND YOU GOLF. "

"NICE TRY, HERB, BUT I'M AFRAID YOU'LL STILL HAVE TO HIT FROM THE MEN'S TEE."

" I CAN'T PLAY WITH THIS BALL, GEORGE! THE COLOR DOESN'T GO WITH MY OUTFIT! "

"AND NOW THAT YOU HAVE ALL THE FACTS IN THE CASE I URGE YOU TO REACH A FAIR, BUT VERY FAST VERDICT."

"PLEASE DON'T ASK HIM ABOUT HIS GOLF GAME."

"WHEN I SAID I COULD MAKE SOME CHANGES IN MY GOLF PLANS TO HELP YOU WITH THE GARDEN, ELAINE, I DIDN'T MEAN,...."

ONE SMALL STEP FOR WOMAN-KIND

76

" YOU'RE TELLING ME WE HAVE DIVERGENT INTERESTS AREN'T YOU, ALICE ? "

" HAVE A GOOD TIME, GEORGE. I'LL JUST SPEND THE AFTERNOON WATCHING A NEW FEATURE ON THE SHOPPING CHANNEL TITLED 'HOW TO GET EVEN WITH YOUR GOLFING HUSBAND'. "

"Y'KNOW, FRAN, I THINK YOU COULD GET A
BETTER GRIP ON THAT RAKE IF YOU USED AN
INTERLOCKING GRIP RATHER THAN AN OVERLAPPING GRIP."

" IT'S A SPORTS RELATED INJURY, HE FELL OFF A
BAR STOOL AT THE 19th HOLE."

"ALL RIGHT, ALL RIGHT, ALICE...I'LL CUT DOWN ON THE GOLF AND SPEND MORE TIME WITH THE KIDS.....WHAT ARE THEIR NAMES ?"

" YOUR CADDY SEEMS TO KNOW YOUR GAME
PRETTY WELL, GEORGE , "

" SOMETHING IN SEPARATE VACATIONS, PERHAPS? "

"AM I TO ASSUME THAT YOU DON'T WANT TO HEAR ABOUT MY BIRDIE ON THE 12TH HOLE, ALICE?"

"SEE GUYS! I TOLD YOU I COULD MAKE A 2:00 TEE OFF TIME!"

"OH, COME ON CHARLIE. WHO IN THE WORLD WOULD GO TO ALL THE TROUBLE OF GOING DOWN TO THE BASEMENT TO GET YOUR GOLF CLUBS, BRING THEM UP HERE TO THE DRIVEWAY AND RUN OVER THEM THREE TIMES WITH MY CAR?"

" BUT, ENOUGH ABOUT MY ROUND OF GOLF. WHATS
NEW WITH YOU, ALICE ? "

"YES, YOU'VE HAD A NUMBER OF TERRIBLE LIES TODAY, GEORGE, NOT THE LEAST OF WHICH IS THE SCORECARD."

92

" WELL, AT LEAST THERE WASN'T A LOT OF DUMB DEBATE ABOUT WHO GOT THE REALLY IMPORTANT STUFF, RIGHT, BERNIE. "

" WELL, THEN .... WOULD YOU BELIEVE A SIX ?"

"HOW COME WHEN IT'S RAINING THIS HARD ON SUNDAYS IT'S RAINING TOO HARD TO GO TO CHURCH?"

"CAN YOU BELIEVE IT, BILL? ALICE WANTED ME TO STAY HOME AND CLEAN THE DOWNSPOUTS ON A MISERABLE DAY LIKE THIS,".

" SAY!....HOW COME OUR BUDGET AXE
NEVER FALLS ON GOLF EQUIPMENT ? "

" STOP COMPLAINING, MARY! YOU'RE THE ONE
WHO SAID I NEVER TAKE YOU ANYWHERE."

"FORESAKING ALL OTHERS DOESN'T INCLUDE WATCHING THE MASTERS ON TELEVISION, ALICE."

"IT WAS THE ONLY WAY I COULD GET HIM TO HELP WITH THE YARD WORK."

"I FINALLY FIGURED OUT WHY HE WORKED SO HARD OVER THE CENTURIES TO LEARN TO STAND ERECT."

" WE MISSED YOU THIS MORNING, MY SON. '

"IT'S GREAT! MY WIFE HAS ALWAYS WANTED A HOUSE NEAR THE GOLF COURSE, HAVEN'T YOU, DEAR."

"CHARLIE HAS ALL THE SHOTS. HE CAN SLICE, HOOK, FADE OR HIT IT STRAIGHT. NONE OF THEM ON PURPOSE, OF COURSE."

"THIS HAS SOMETHING TO DO WITH THE TIME I SPENT ON THE GOLF COURSE THIS SUMMER DOESN'T IT?"

"BEING MARRIED TO A TRIPLE-BOGIE SEEMS TO BE PAR FOR MY COURSE."

" THE IRONS WERE SUPPOSED TO BE A NEW REFRIGERATOR, THE WOODS WERE SUPPOSED TO BE A NEW LAWN MOWER, THE SHOES WERE SUPPOSED TO BE... "

".. AND THIS IS A DIVOT FROM HARRY'S ROUND AT PEBBLE BEACH IN 1993."

"TOM PRIDES HIMSELF ON THE FACT THAT HE'S NEVER HAD A GOLF LESSON."

" WHEN I SAID I WANTED A NEW IRON
FOR MY BIRTHDAY, GEORGE ...."

" IT ALL STARTED WHEN HE STOPPED PLAYING GOLF ON SUNDAY MORNINGS. "